HOW DOES IT WORK?: FA
COMBINES

by Johannah Luza

pogo

Ideas for Parents and Teachers

Pogo Books let children practice reading informational text while introducing them to nonfiction features such as headings, labels, sidebars, maps, and diagrams, as well as a table of contents, glossary, and index.

Carefully leveled text with a strong photo match offers early fluent readers the support they need to succeed.

Before Reading

- "Walk" through the book and point out the various nonfiction features. Ask the student what purpose each feature serves.
- Look at the glossary together. Read and discuss the words.

Read the Book

- Have the child read the book independently.
- Invite him or her to list questions that arise from reading.

After Reading

- Discuss the child's questions. Talk about how he or she might find answers to those questions.
- Prompt the child to think more. Ask: How do combines help farmers harvest crops efficiently?

Pogo Books are published by Jump!
5357 Penn Avenue South
Minneapolis, MN 55419
www.jumplibrary.com

Library of Congress Cataloging-in-Publication Data

Names: Luza, Johannah, author.
Title: Combines / by Johannah Luza.
Description: Minneapolis, MN: Jump!, Inc., [2024]
Series: How does it work? Farm tech | Includes index.
Audience: Ages 7-10
Identifiers: LCCN 2023000222 (print)
LCCN 2023000223 (ebook)
ISBN 9798885246859 (hardcover)
ISBN 9798885246866 (paperback)
ISBN 9798885246873 (ebook)
Subjects: LCSH: Combines
(Agricultural machinery) –Juvenile literature.
Classification: LCC S696 .L89 2024 (print)
LCC S696 (ebook)
DDC 631.3/7–dc23/eng/20230105
LC record available at https://lccn.loc.gov/2023000222
LC ebook record available at https://lccn.loc.gov/2023000223
LC ebook record available at https://lccn.loc.gov/2022023614

Editor: Eliza Leahy
Designer: Emma Almgren-Bersie
Content Consultant: Santosh K. Pitla, Ph.D.,
Biological Systems Engineering

Photo Credits: Nicholas Smith/iStock, cover, 10-11; Radu Cadar/Shutterstock, 1; Ortodox/Shutterstock, 3; Image Source/iStock, 4; goikmitl/iStock, 5; smereka/Shutterstock, 6-7; Arctic ice/Shutterstock, 8; Pierre BRYE/Alamy, 9; Panoramic Images/Alamy, 12-13; Joseph Kreiss/Shutterstock, 14-15; MC MEDIASTUDIO/Shutterstock, 16; National Farmers Union/Alamy, 17; vbacarin/iStock, 18-19; recep-bg/iStock, 20-21; Anatoliy Kosolapov/Shutterstock, 23.

Printed in the United States of America at Corporate Graphics in North Mankato, Minnesota.

TABLE OF CONTENTS

CHAPTER 1

WHAT IS A COMBINE?

What do you eat for breakfast? Is it cereal, toast, or oatmeal? These foods are all made from grains.

wheat field

Grains grow in fields as **crops**. Corn and beans are food crops, too. Cotton is another crop. It is made into **textiles**.

Farmers use combines to **harvest** crops from fields. These big machines help farmers collect a lot of crops quickly.

DID YOU KNOW?

Farmers once cut crops with hand tools. It took a long time. In the 1800s, a family could harvest two acres (8,100 square meters) a day. Today, combines help farmers harvest around 200 acres (810,000 sq m) a day.

CHAPTER 2

HOW DO COMBINES WORK?

We can only eat parts of some crops. For example, only a wheat plant's seeds are made into grains we eat. Combines help with this. How? They separate seeds from the rest of the plant.

wheat seed

As a combine drives, the head gathers crops. The reel pushes the crops to the cutter bar. This part acts like teeth. It cuts the crops.

cutter bar

Cut crops go up the conveyor. The threshin drum shakes the grains off their **stalks**. The grains fall through **sieves**. They go into the grain tank. The unwanted parts pass along straw walkers.

TAKE A LOOK!

What are the parts of a combine? Take a look!

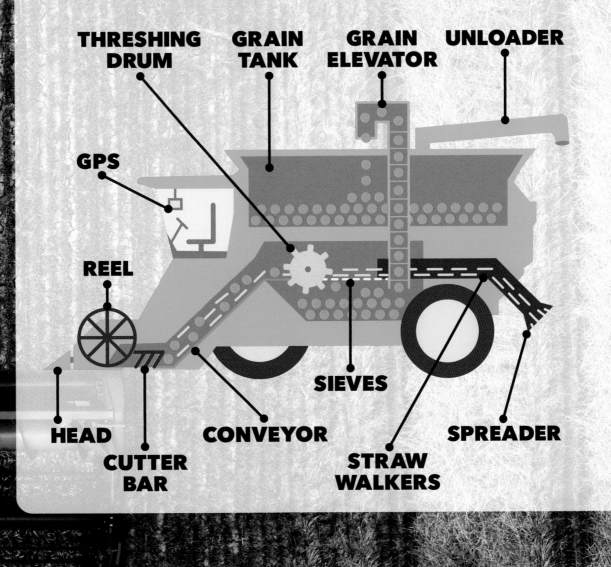

THRESHING DRUM

GRAIN TANK

GRAIN ELEVATOR

UNLOADER

GPS

REEL

HEAD

CUTTER BAR

CONVEYOR

SIEVES

STRAW WALKERS

SPREADER

When the tank is full, grain shoots out of the unloader. It pours into a grain cart. The unwanted parts fall out the back of the combine. The spreader spreads them over the land.

tractor ····▶

unloader

grain
cart

Different kinds of crops need different combine heads. Why? Different plants have different parts. Heads separate the parts of the plant.

A head for harvesting corn has big prongs called snouts. The snouts break corn ears from the stalks and pull the ears into the combine.

DID YOU KNOW?

Inside a corn combine, the husks, kernels, and cobs are separated. The kernels are stored. The cobs and husks are spit back onto the ground.

snout

CHAPTER 3

NEW TECH

Today, fewer people farm. But we need more food. Why? The world's **population** is growing. New technology is helping us harvest more.

GPS gives farmers information. How? As a combine drives over a field, **sensors** find **moisture** in the soil. They also sense how much sunlight crops are getting. This helps farmers decide which areas are best to grow crops. GPS also reads how much grain is being harvested.

GPS

GPS maps the land. This helps farmers work in difficult conditions. These can include darkness, rain, dust, and fog. GPS also helps farmers drive around hills and uneven ground.

Farmers use apps to help run combines. The apps can find **mechanical** problems. They can suggest how to fix the problem.

The world is changing. So are combines. They are more **efficient** than ever. This is important. Why? They harvest crops to feed people around the world!

DID YOU KNOW?

By 2024, new combines may drive on their own. This would allow farmers more time for other tasks.

ACTIVITIES & TOOLS

COLLECT MORE CROPS

Large combine heads with more prongs collect more crops. See how with this fun activity!

What You Need:
- popsicle sticks
- golf tees
- glue
- corn kernels
- paper
- pencil

❶ Lie one popsicle stick down flat. Glue another popsicle stick on top to make a T with the two sticks.

❷ With the sticks still lying flat, glue the tops of three golf tees to the top stick. Glue one on each end and one in the middle. The points should stick up. Let the rake dry.

❸ Pour the corn kernels in a pile.

❹ Drag the rake through the pile. How many corn kernels does it gather? Count them, and record the number.

❺ Now, glue two more prongs to the rake head. After it dries, rake through a new pile of corn kernels. How many kernels does it gather?

❻ Compare how many kernels the 3-prong and 5-prong rake collected. How is this like a combine head?

GLOSSARY

crops: Plants grown for food or profit.

efficient: Working very well and not wasting time or energy.

harvest: To gather crops from a field.

mechanical: Of or having to do with machines or engines.

mills: Buildings that contain machinery for grinding grain into flour.

moisture: Wetness from rain, snow, dew, or fog.

population: The total number of people who live in a place.

sensors: Tools that can find and measure changes and send the information to a controlling device.

sieves: Containers consisting of wire or plastic mesh in a frame, used for separating large pieces from small pieces.

stalks: The main stems of plants from which leaves and flowers grow.

textiles: Woven or knitted fabrics.

TO LEARN MORE

Finding more information is as easy as 1, 2, 3.

❶ Go to www.factsurfer.com

❷ Enter "combines" into the search box.

❸ Choose your book to see a list of websites.

FACT SURFER